Bibliographical Series
of Supplements to ' British Book News '

★

GENERAL EDITOR
T. O. Beachcroft

SIR OSBERT SITWELL
from a photograph by BILL BRANDT

OSBERT
SITWELL

By ROGER FULFORD

PUBLISHED FOR

THE BRITISH COUNCIL

and the NATIONAL BOOK LEAGUE

BY LONGMANS, GREEN & CO., LONDON, NEW YORK, TORONTO

LONGMANS, GREEN & CO. LTD.
6 & 7 Clifford Street, London, W.1
Also at Melbourne and Cape Town

LONGMANS, GREEN & CO. INC.
55 Fifth Avenue, New York, 3

LONGMANS, GREEN & CO.
215 Victoria Street, Toronto, 1

ORIENT LONGMANS LTD.
Bombay, Calcutta, Madras

First published in 1951

*Printed in Great Britain by Benham and Company Limited
Colchester*

OSBERT SITWELL

I

COLERIDGE, by way of illustrating the restricted vision of the human race, once remarked that to most men 'experience is like the stern lights of a ship which illumine only the track it has passed '.[1] Among such men Osbert Sitwell can certainly not be numbered. His own experience of life, the recollection of which is among the most important and constant elements in all his writing, reveals not merely his own path but lights up with fascinating brilliance the unexpected and unexplored which lie all round. This achievement is the more significant when it is remembered that his background was conventional and that the setting for his early years was not one from which might be expected the development of imaginative gifts.

He was born in 1892 and his father, Sir George Sitwell, Bt., was the head of a family long established and with large territorial possessions in Derbyshire. His mother, Lady Ida, was the daughter of Lord Londesborough, and the great-grand-daughter of the Marchioness Conyngham, the lady whose company was a solace to King George IV in his declining years. His home, Renishaw, had all the spacious magnificence of the traditional English country house. In addition he spent some of his boyhood and youth in Scarborough—one of those watering places in which were still to be found, like the last rats lingering in the rafters of a doomed barn, those curious survivals of Victorian times who rustle so vividly through some of Sir Osbert's works. As was the inexorable fashion for boys of his standing Osbert Sitwell went (in 1903) to a preparatory school. This school was kept by a famous amateur footballer, known as 'the tremendous dribbler', and was described by Sir Osbert as 'a miniature model prison'.[2] On leaving his private school he went to Eton, a school which (with characteristically mordant wit) he said that he liked, except

[1] S. T. Coleridge, *Table Talk*.
[2] *The Scarlet Tree*. Macmillan 1946, p. 126.

in the following respects : ' for work and games, for boys and masters '.[1] English school-life, which in those years set much store upon the extinction of individuality, upon games and upon discomfort, was naturally wholly antipathetic to him. After he left Eton he served in the British Army as an Officer in the Brigade of Guards, fighting with his regiment in France in the war of 1914.

At the outset it is essential to stress the point that although his surroundings and upbringing were typical of the upper classes in Edwardian England, they were lifted out of the commonplace by the remarkable family to which he belonged. Though, as will be shown later, it might be easy to dismiss his father, Sir George, as an eccentric, this would be shallow and mistaken ; he had decided literary gifts and if he must have been at times an aggravating parent he was certainly a stimulating and amusing influence in developing the intellectual curiosity of his children. His mother was singularly affectionate and warmhearted. Of all the mothers depositing their offspring in ' the model prison ' she, with a disregard for appearances which was typical of the English aristocracy, was the only one to indulge in unashamed tears. To have had a sister like Miss Edith Sitwell must have been a perpetual refreshment—her magnetic genius ever serving to draw her brother's mind away from all that was dim and dreary. Though he was separated by five years from his younger brother, Sacheverell, they were constant companions ; from earliest youth he delighted in the quick and merry flashes of his younger brother's intelligence. For many young people, high spirited and witty, Scarborough would have been a sarcophagus of boredom. Yet instead of grumbling and grousing at their hard lot, kicking their heels and cursing the curious odds and ends of humanity which formed ' Society ' at this watering place, they appraised and observed. Perhaps the finest fruits of this observation are to be found in the opening story of *Triple Fugue*, which was published in 1924.   Sir

[1] *The Scarlet Tree*, p. 257.

Osbert is describing the crowd gathered round the Winter Garden band as it plays selections from *The Geisha* and other tinkling little tunes from the musical comedies of the day— the military gentlemen with their elbows out-turned, the elderly ladies, ' grey haired, broad based, who, if they move, sway a little from side to side like ducks on their way to the pond ', the bath-chairs which ' look like the gigantic shells of ocean snails '. Into this distinguished company the Misses Cantrell-Cooksey made their belated entry. ' They were bedizened and a-jingle with little crinkling ornaments, ruby bars, gold bangles, slave bracelets, small watches set with half-pearls hanging from enamelled brooches shaped like true lover's knots : they were decked out with little pieces of lace, numerous ribbons, and a thousand other joyous trifles.' No intelligent reader could fail to notice the penetrating observation on which these sketches are based and the enjoyment which the author must have derived from their study. They never merge into harsh-ness because Sir Osbert, like Mr. Bennett in *Pride and Prejudice* never loses sight of the common bonds of oddity which link mankind. ' For what do we live, but to make sport for our neighbours and laugh at them in our turn ? '

There are two other points in connexion with Sir Osbert's early days which any student of his writing will be careful to observe. The first of these is the subject of an admirable sentence in *Laughter in the Next Room*—' I belonged by birth, education, nature, outlook, and period to the pre-war era, a proud citizen of the great free world of 1914, in which comity prevailed '.[1] Many acute minds, looking back to the shining years of their early life, have felt almost a sense of privilege in having been allowed to live in a period of tranquil splendour. Perhaps Talleyrand first gave expression to this idea when he wrote, ' They who did not live before 1789 knew not the sweetness of life '. Sir Osbert has gone even further and has derived from his early years a sense of detachment, even of superiority, as, recollecting the

[1] *Laughter in the Next Room.* Macmillan 1949, p. 249.

past, he surveys the years of waste and chaos through which the world is now moving.

The other point is his sense of affinity with working men and women—in other words with all who are creating something. He rightly draws a distinction between himself and the ' city-bred, middle-class poets of the proletarian movement ' who regretfully feel that they are cut off from the working classes.[1] For Sir Osbert such barriers do not exist : the only barrier of which he is conscious is that between the creative class and the absorbing class. Once again this sense of alliance with men of action and creative gifts (perhaps illustrated by the dedication of one of his volumes of autobiography to Field-Marshal Lord Alexander) gives to his writing the ring of confidence and authority.

Yet the start of his working career was not to be easy. He was twenty-one when on an evening in August 1914 he stood in the Mall looking towards Buckingham Palace and as he shrewdly expresses it ' heard the great crowd roar for its own death '.[2] The effect of war on him was to rouse him to a sense of frustrated fury with the older generation who were in some measure responsible, and with all who, engaged in the humdrum task of keeping the home fires burning, were too easily comforted by the trite banalities and silly clichés of the newspaper men.

> Then the red dawn came
> —And no thought touched me
> Except pity, anger
> And bitter reproach.
> God filled my mouth
> With the burning pebbles of hatred,
> And choked my soul
> With a whirl-wind of fury . . .
> I ridiculed them,
> I despised them,
> I loathed them.[3]

[1] *Left Hand ! Right Hand !* Macmillan 1945, p. x.
[2] *Great Morning.* Macmillan 1948, p. 297.
[3] *Collected Satires and Poems of Osbert Sitwell.* Duckworth 1931, p. 7.

His impatience of the humbug of patriotism is perhaps nowhere better seen than in the poem ' Rhapsode '. What G. K. Chesterton once described as ' the easy speeches that comfort cruel men ' were revealed in all their naked horror by the devastating lines

> We know you now—and what you wish to be told ;
> That the larks are singing in the trenches,
> That the fruit trees will again blossom in the spring,
> That Youth is always happy.[1]

Like all the young men of his generation he was doomed to watch the obliteration of his circle of companions and friends. For him, as indeed for many with perceptive insight into this tragedy, the sense of loss was sharpened by a feeling of despair against those who carried on at home in rich, insensitive oblivion. As he expressed it not unjustly—though possibly too fiercely for every taste—

> Or those who rich and old,
> Have battened on the slaughter,
> Whose faces, gorged with blood and gold,
> Are creased in purple laughter![2]

Many of these powerful poems written during the closing years of the war were designed to rouse people out of the fallacy of regarding the war as something to be accepted with fatalism and to be waged, as the lawyers say, in perpetuity. 'Rhapsode', which was published a few weeks before the former Foreign Secretary, Lord Lansdowne, made his public appeal for a negotiated peace, ends with the suggestion that the state of the nation was so topsyturvy that to want peace was a short cut to the prison house or lunatic asylum. The poem was dedicated to H. W. Massingham, who was editing the *Nation* (the leading journal of advanced and independent thinking at the time, in which many of Sir Osbert's early poems were published) ; he was the warm advocate of a negotiated peace.

Sir Osbert has himself told us that from the moment he

[1] *Collected Satires and Poems*, p. 14.
[2] op. cit., p. 19.

began to write, even in the middle of a world war, his life
found a purpose. In 1916 he was sent back to England as
the result of severe illness, and for the closing months of the
war he was able to give more time to writing and to
mixing with less orthodox writers than he had previously
met. His reputation as a writer of forceful, satirical poetry
was established and increasing by 1918. After the war was
finished there was plenty of opportunity for developing and
sharpening this gift. To this period belong two distinguished poems, 'The Winstonburg Line', an attack on the
ill-conceived effort to invade Russia in 1920, and 'How
shall we Rise to Greet the Dawn', which was written at the
time of the Armistice. In somewhat similar vein was the
splendid series of poems about Mrs. Kinfoot, which was
intended to expose the flabby follies of the British *bour-
geois* classes. One of these poems, 'At the house of Mrs.
Kinfoot', contained the lines which are often quoted

> The British Bourgeoisie,
> Is not born,
> And does not die,
> But, if it is ill,
> It has a frightened look in its eyes.[1]

From the point of view of English literary history much
interest attaches to his satirical attack (reminiscent of Pope)
on J. C. Squire and the Georgian poets. This was called
'the Jolly Old Squire' or 'Way Down Georgia'.

Before dealing with the more developed examples of Sir
Osbert's work we may pause to consider one aspect
of this work of his earlier period, much of which was
satirical. In his novel *Miracle on Sinai*,[2] which was, of course,
published much later, he wrote of one of the characters,
'Nevertheless, however occasionally absurd, a person and a
writer of distinction. Again whatever may be urged
against him or his theories, at least he had understood that
something was wrong ; but he had *felt* it with the heart of

[1] *Collected Satires and Poems,* p. 64.
[2] *Miracle on Sinai.* Duckworth 1933, p. 34.

the poet instead of with the intuition of a prophet and teacher.' Though time would possibly soften some of Sir Osbert's verdicts on his contemporaries in those early 1920's, like the character of his own creation in *Miracle on Sinai*, he saw that something was wrong. But unlike that character he saw both as poet and prophet. He was from the start—and he still is to-day—a writer with vision.

But it would be a mistake in considering his poetry to suppose that beauty and poetic feeling are completely jostled out by wit and satire. To go back to Pope—many people think of him only as the scourge of the literary dolts and dullards of his generation : they forget, for example, his beautiful Pastorals. So with Sir Osbert. The beauty of such a poem as ' Winter The Huntsman ',[1] the splendid imagery in ' Fox Trot '[2] (When Solomon Met the Queen of Sheba), and the powers of imagination in the opening lines of ' Cornucopia '[3] will be missed by no sensitive reader. Nor could readers study his short poem 'Night' without sensing that they were enjoying poetry of a singularly high order. After retailing all the haunting sorrows and dim terrors of an ancient house at night he sums them up with the lines,

> These are the signs the Gods have given us
> To know the limits of our days and powers.[4]

His devotion to his sister Edith and the feeling that he, in close alliance with her and his brother, are together battling for truth and beauty were admirably expressed in the poem of dedication to his sister,

> To you, who earn the ever-righteous hate
> Of crowds of giggling, chic cads, I dedicate
> These memories of a time when children three
> We walked all winter by the white-winged sea,
> And under shelter of its lion voice,
> Proclaimed the name of Beauty, made our choice.[5]

[1] *Collected Satires and Poems*, p. 116.
[2] op. cit., p. 142.
[3] op. cit., p. 154.
[4] op. cit., p. 165.
[5] op. cit., p. 195.

II

During the 1920's Sir Osbert published three important books of prose—*Triple Fugue* in 1924, *Discursions on Travel, Art and Life* in 1925, and *Before the Bombardment* in 1927. *Triple Fugue* consists of six long studies of human behaviour and of human eccentricity—an amusing and fascinating collection. But the reader will notice the serious motive lying behind this book : his purpose here has been well defined as 'to satirize the scientific, political, and social tendencies which seem to him to-day to threaten individuality in a machine-run civilization'.[1] The threat of 1924 has moved perceptibly nearer in 1951 and that is perhaps one of the reasons why Sir Osbert's prose writings keep their sparkle and freshness.

Before the Bombardment, undoubtedly, after the autobiography, Sir Osbert's finest book, is a satirical novel and describes Scarborough before 1914, and the unexpected shelling of the town by German cruisers at the close of that year. It portrays that curious twilight existence of British commercial prosperity in which the great fortunes of the Victorian money-making classes had fallen massively on widows and spinster daughters who, in the drab society of companions and confidential servants, were beating out their comfortable lives in residential hotels within sound of where the ' splintering steel rollers thudded at the town all day, and hammered, muffled by wind, all the night long, as though secretly preparing for it a coffin. . . .'[2] He himself has described it as 'the foundation of my whole reputation'.

Discursions is a most memorable and original account of Southern Italy and some parts of Germany.

These books were followed by two novels—*The Man who Lost Himself*, 1929, and *Miracle on Sinai*, 1933, and a volume of short stories, *Dumb Animal*, 1930.

These six books out of the corpus of Sir Osbert's writings

[1] *The Three Sitwells*. R. L. Mégroz. Richards Press 1927, p. 203.
[2] *Before the Bombardment*. Duckworth, sixth impression, pp. 66-7.

afford the modern reader an excellent platform from which to survey the qualities of his work before they reached their full maturity during the later 1930's and 1940's.

The reader will remember his poem dedicated to his sister and the ringing line with which it closes,

> Proclaimed the name of Beauty, made our choice.

That intellectual passion for beauty enlivens and colours all his work. It explains why a somewhat mundane writer like Arnold Bennett, reviewing one of Sir Osbert's poems, was shaken out of himself and wrote, ' Lo ! he is now creating ideal beauty '. This statement (possibly expressed in less fervent language) could certainly be applied to almost all Sir Osbert's prose writings. On every page the reader becomes conscious of the author's intellectual passion for beauty. This is predominant even in the description of things and events which must have been inevitably anti-pathetic to him. For example, his description of the cricket match at the Newborough Festival certainly deserves to rank with the account of a more conventional match which has found its way into *The Oxford Book of English Prose*. Sir Osbert writes, ' At first the game was very silent, except for the drawing-room conversation of bat and ball ; this wooden small-talk would proceed for some time, and then, suddenly, one of the talkers would snub the other, and away would run the fat white mice over the flat green baize '.[1]

Again and again Sir Osbert shows that this intellectual feeling for beauty is combined to a striking extent with the sensitiveness of the artist. Anyone familiar with his books, allowing their minds to travel back in recollection, can see before them the bleak greyness of Scarborough or the splendours of Renishaw in high summer depicted with all the faithful skill of a master. In his books, as Wordsworth remarked of another artist, is to be found

> Spirit-moving imagery
> Intensely studied with a painter's eye,
> A poet's heart.

[1] *Before the Bombardment*, p. 239.

Perhaps next to his artistic perception must be placed his powers of description. They are shown at their most vivid in English scenes but they are hardly less excellent on unfamiliar scenery such as the desert in *Miracle on Sinai*. For instance, he has a most agreeable passage on the competition in noise between the singing in the chapel and the countless soft noises of the desert—'the natural crepitations of the desert, that shifting and singing of myriads of grains of sand moved by the faintest wind, and the continual expansion and contractions imposed upon every object by the heat, waxing or waning, of the sun, and which, if we could hear them in their entirety, instead of being but here a rustle and there a creak, would form a regular though ever-modified song of life, superb but intimidating '.[1]

In a short but admirable sketch of Charles Dickens[2] which he published in 1932 he wrote of Dickens's ' courageous observation which verged continually on prophecy '. He no doubt particularly had in mind those social evils which Dickens so minutely described and of whose amelioration he was, in some measure, the herald. That is also largely true of Sir Osbert's own gifts of observation and description. For example, in *Miracle on Sinai* he describes with almost faultless wit representative and respected types who flourished in England between the two wars. Among these are the newspaper magnate who modelled himself on Napoleon—or more precisely on what he conceived Napoleon to have been, which was a species of circusking ; the publicity-hunting bishop who composed the special prayers to be read in all places of worship on the Day of National Prayer for the Recovery of the Pound ; Sir Levy Lollygo, a Jewish financier who had taken the British Empire under his black wing, and who was always contriving to fill the newspapers with the sage advice that ' We must learn to think imperially ' ; Sir Levy's elegant daughter Miss Poppy, who was met by a newspaperman ' at a

[1] *Miracle on Sinai*, p. 24.
[2] *Dickens*, by Osbert Sitwell. Chatto & Windus, 1932.

little pyjama cocktail party she threw in the Aaron Palace Hotel'; and described 'the lovely little villa which she and her father had built outside Bethlehem . . . all the old beams were sent from England, and so was the furniture as well as numerous flowers'; Lady Helen Hornmaker, 'the greatest ornament of our Divorce Courts, who was conducting a dressmaking establishment'. Such types and characters made by the chit-chat columns of newspapers into the familiars of countless British homes were at once the leaders of certain sections of British social life between the wars and the portents of its doom. Today they are ridiculous and pathetic : then they were honoured and aped. Prophet-like Sir Osbert sets them in their brittle absurdity—obvious enough to-day—rather than in their glory of twenty years ago when he was writing.

In his journal,[1] Arnold Bennett makes a striking observation about Sir Osbert. He describes how he was given a copy of *Before the Bombardment* and how it carried the splendid inscription from the author, 'To dear good Uncle Arnold from a nephew' : he then adds rather tartly, 'the man *describes* characters instead of showing them'. For a novelist like Bennett the idea of breaking the tradition of the modern English novel by which character is developed rather than revealed was surprising and shocking. No doubt judged simply as novels in the twentieth-century manner both *Miracle on Sinai* and *Before the Bombardment* would fall short of what was expected. But even Bennett noticed at once the author's power to describe character. In this respect he is in line with Dickens, whose power of vivifying a character by description has never been matched. At times Sir Osbert recalls Dickens in this particular. An instance from a much later book is Sir Oswald's account of Julian Field, the swindler who extracted money from his mother. This recalls Dickens at his most powerful : 'His stunted, stooping, paunchy body, with over-delicate hands and feet, carried a heavy head, as though he

[1] *Journal of Arnold Bennett*, iii, 162.

was wearing a mask with a beak like that of an octopus which spiritually he so much resembled, and a small imperial and moustache that were dyed, as was his hair, a total and unnatural black.... As a rule—and I saw him several times —he wore striped trousers, a frock-coat, and a grey top-hat that, like his face, had acquired a tinge of yellow in it from wear, or as if in some way tainted. In the street, as he walked, at a rather slow, self-important pace, he would glance shiftily from side to side, nervous no doubt of meeting some of the hundreds of victims he had black-mailed and squeezed in his time. . . ."[1] The picture is brilliantly clear, nothing is savage or harsh, but with a minimum of exaggeration the thrill of expectant horror is created.

Even in these earlier books, written at the start of his career, there is plenty of evidence of his patient scholarship. That is a word which in modern literary parlance has acquired a decidedly precious ring and is too often bandied about by complacent commentators to excuse the dullness of a book. Sir Osbert's scholarship is not of this order and it might perhaps be fairer to describe it as distinction of mind. It is tolerably safe to say that in any two pages of any of these books will be found some little pocket or crevice filled with information of an unusual and arresting character. In *Triple Fugue*, one of the men is described as having ' an enchanting shutting of one eye, opening of the other, such as were introduced as the symbols of Upper and Lower Egypt into the ceremonial mummification of dead Pharaohs '.[2] In *Discursions* we learn that King Bomba of Naples, whose rule was described by Mr. Gladstone as ' the negation of God ', died in great agony from the same loathsome disease as laid low King Herod.[3] Anyone ignorant of the nature of King Herod's last illness will enjoy a fascinating voyage of discovery through dictionaries,

---

[1] *Great Morning*, 162–2.
[2] *Triple Fugue*. Grant Richards, 1924, p. 154.
[3] *Discursions*. Grant Richards, 1925, p. 46.

encyclopaedias, and the Acts of the Apostles. Even when he is ridiculing the foibles of a character he relieves any possible monotony by enriching the story with stray pieces of information which (in spite of their setting) the reader suspects to be true to life. An illustration of this is to be found in *Miracle on Sinai*, where the wife of a great pro-consul of Empire announces that 'Indian princes are very nervous and frightened of pain (you know what they're like —quite different from us)'.[1] Throughout these books he shows that he has the gift (possessed perhaps pre-eminently by Edward Fitzgerald) of decking out even the most trifling objects with their little paraphernalia of wit and learning. As Dr. Johnson said of Burke, 'the stream of his mind is perpetual'.

Some other points in Sir Osbert's style are also worthy of notice. He had—even in these early prose writings—the arresting habit of rounding off an amusing episode with a pointed and often sombre reflection. Like Lloyd George and all accomplished orators he rouses his audience with a quip and then drives home the point he seeks to make. There is an example of this in *Discursions* where he is describing his journey from Covent Garden in a three-wheeled hansom cab. He was conscious of faces gazing at him with amused interest. This happened shortly before August 1914, and he adds that the eccentric cab and its driver 'no doubt in the general rush to make the world safe for democracy . . . have vanished, or are only retained in the petrifying crystal of our memories, to die when we die'.[2] In somewhat the same fashion he describes the death of a young soldier in the trenches and after telling of his youthful rustic grace he suddenly asks, 'Who else living remembers him to-day, I wonder?'[3] The reader, following his train of thought, imagines some cottage home where the boy's memory is still treasured, or pictures the youth's home circle

[1] *Miracle on Sinai*, p. 225.
[2] *Discursions*, p. 18.
[3] *Laughter in the Next Room*, p. 85.

scattered by death, and recalls the Preacher's vivid words in the Old Testament about a man's life leaving no track behind it.

In these six books one further characteristic of this writer is clearly marked, and that is a certain spaciousness of outlook, a concentration on detail, which gives to those who read him a delightful sense of leisure. He takes a piece of scenery or a character and displays them for us with the thoroughness of a modiste who fingers her creations and is seemingly reluctant to part from them. Here, for example, is the account of Miss Waddington, one of the grandees of Newborough, on the morning of the Bombardment :

> It was a dull morning in the first December of the Great War and Miss Waddington, then in her 87th year was sitting propped up in bed at 8.30 before a creditable breakfast of tea, toast, poached eggs and marmalade. The local newspaper was by her side. So Mrs. Sibmarshe's son had been killed ! Well, one could never have foreseen that. But here her attention was drawn away by the intruding damp coldness of the morning—a rather unusual morning for the time of year it seemed to her ; though foggy and cold, there was for once no sound of embattled wind and wave. It was chilly, the old lady observed, distinctly chilly in spite of the fire, and she was just asking for an extra shawl (the light blue one in shell-stitch) when, quite without warning, death darted at her from the sea, and Miss Waddington, and her bedroom with her, was pulverized, fading with a swift, raucous whistling and crashing into the murky air.[1]

III

Before going on to consider Sir Osbert's later writings, we may examine his standing in that unsatisfactory, protracted drop-scene between the two wars. After the end of the 1914 war, as the captain in the Grenadier Guards merged into the private citizen, he took leave of his military life with characteristic and amusing gestures. The news of his final demobilization reached him when he was in the

[1] *Before the Bombardment*, p. 310.

South of France and from here he launched his uniform in a hamper out to sea.   His bearskin was made into a muff for his housekeeper.

Throughout these years he was a harsh and not ineffective critic of the complacent follies of his age.   The triumph of democracy, which was supposed to have followed the war and which was proclaimed by national leaders and accepted with docile gratitude by the people, was possibly more truly characterized by Sir Osbert as ' the popular reign of piracy . . . the world in which the sabre-toothed tiger and the ant are our paragons, and the butterfly is condemned for its wings, which are uneconomic '.[1]

Unlike some critics of the time, the Sitwells did not withdraw and croak from afar their disapproval of the foolishness of their fellows.   Sir Osbert's writings are full of warnings, full of ridicule for the half-truths and the trite and comfortable sayings by which men and women sought to protect themselves from the cold winds of reality.   He was no hermit: he led a life of fashion, of travel, and of intellectual diversion.   He found his enjoyment among the more intelligent members of the aristocracy who, in those years, much frequented the houses and parties of a number of wealthy, good natured (though not especially accomplished) ladies.   His name was observed in the Court Circular as staying with King George and Queen Elizabeth at Windsor Castle.   The social habits of the Englishmen were changing.   Gone were the days of the dawn of the twentieth century, when the British aristocrat thought of little except killing something furred or feathered, the flash of cards or an uncomfortable practical joke.   The full horror of those times is realistically described by Sir Osbert in his autobiography.   In the years between the wars English Society recovered something of its old splendour but shed many of its old frivolities.   A man of attainments and standing in literature like Sir Osbert was consequently warmly welcomed in fashionable circles.

[1] *Laughter in the Next Room*, pp. 5–6.

There is always the risk that a writer who is known to mingle in social life will stir the jealousy of his brethren and invite the charitable stricture that he must be lazy. Some-one once accused Sir Osbert of being lazy in the hearing of Arnold Bennett. After an explosive fit of laughing Bennett observed, 'The truth with Osbert is that he has seven pro-fessions, not one, and a life devoted to each'. During these years he was writer, traveller, politician, pamphleteer, editor, and organizer of picture exhibitions. If these did not amount to seven professions they certainly justified the exaggeration. He himself has said that he applied himself to life 'with fury'.[1]

Reading his early prose writings many people might have supposed that in private life he must be peppery and formid-able. In fact he is by nature exceptionally kindly ; count-less people seeking to make their mark in the world of literature have been cheered by the encouragement and interest in their work which he has shown. At a time when the cliques and animosities of writers were singularly strong he stood aloof, feared perhaps by some but respected for his integrity and independence by all. At the beginning of these years the Bloomsbury Group, whose leaders were Roger Fry, Virginia Woolf, Clive Bell, Vanessa Bell, Lytton Strachey, and Duncan Grant, was a potent and exclusive force in Art and Letters. In *Laughter in the Next Room* will be found a critical though not unsym-pathetic picture of Bloomsbury with its accomplished leaders and devoted but less accomplished camp followers who aped the voice and mannerisms of those leaders whose wit and talents they envied but did not share. But although he was friendly with members of the Bloomsbury Circle Sir Osbert was wisely not inside it.[2]

Perhaps the writers with whom he was closest in the years immediately after 1918 were a small group with which he used to have a weekly dinner. The *habitués* here were Sir

[1] *Laughter in the Next Room*, p. 27.
[2] op. cit., pp. 16–17.

Osbert, his brother and sister, Ezra Pound, T. S. Eliot, Herbert Read, and Wyndham Lewis. But increasingly as the 1920's wore on, the Sitwell family was regarded as standing for certain ideals in the Arts and to them the younger generation increasingly looked. This was made apparent at the time of the first production, in the mid-1920's, of *Façade*, a recitation of Edith Sitwell's poems to the accompaniment of music composed by Mr. William Walton. Although the extraordinary, childish, and vulgar outburst with which this was received belongs more strictly to the life of Miss Sitwell it had the effect of rousing interest in all the members of the family, of stimulating admiration and—inevitably enough—of producing groans and squawks from the conventional Philistines. An enlightened genera-tion of undergraduates at Oxford, under the leadership of Mr. Harold Acton, was in close touch with the family on whom it counted for the warfare against the dim and shoddy who, at that time, were all powerful in the world of taste. In the entry which he compiled for *Who's Who*, Sir Osbert has expressed the battle in the following terms : ' For the past twenty-five years has conducted, in con-junction with his brother and sister, a series of skirmishes and hand-to-hand battles against the Philistines. Though outnumbered, has occasionally succeeded in denting the line, though not without damage to himself.'

Although looking back to those years from the comfort-able vantage point of the ground which was won, the reader may think it was easy to battle for certain high principles in Art and Literature ; the struggle was in fact arduous and at times disheartening. *Façade* was politely dismissed by one of the London newspapers as ' drivel ' and another Press columnist was sufficiently broadminded to urge that ' this sort of thing should be stopped '.[1]

Hardly less startling were the comments on *Before the Bombardment*. One of the more popular critics in the Sunday newspapers said that the author had spat on the

[1] *Laughter in the Next Room*, p. 194.

whole of the Victorian Age and that the book ought to
have been called *Great Expectorations*. The *Yorkshire
Post*—at that time the exponent of a particularly peppery
type of provincial conservatism—described the book as
'merely caddish'. Mayors and rectors piped up in
feeble wrath against something which struck them as
violating their peculiarly dreary standards of good taste.
One of the few contemporary writers to acclaim the book
was that gifted, sensitive novelist Mary Webb. She said—
and it was a singularly shrewd remark—that although she
was familiar with the author's poems she had not realized
his 'reserves of intensity'. To us, reading the crackling
satire of *Before the Bombardment* which springs from
gaiety and not from malice, it seems almost incredible
(though indicative of the debased standards against which
Sir Osbert was battling) that writers of standing should have
received it with grim and humourless disfavour. Only the
most superficial reading could detect in *Before the Bombardment* those faults with which Sir Osbert was charged.
A careful and discriminating reader will immediately sense
the pity which lies behind the wit and satire. He parades
his characters before us—the German maid, the companion,
the rich and gossipy old ladies—but we can almost hear the
author's whispered comment as he draws our smile—'*pauvre
humanité*'.

Yet the public attacks on *Before the Bombardment* brought
their private consolations. Shortly after its publication, a
luncheon was organized in his honour ; seventy people
attended, among whom were the giants of those days—
H. G. Wells, Arnold Bennett, Edmund Gosse, Siegfried
Sassoon, and Augustine Birrell.

Many young writers have to pass through the ordeal of
the sententious disapproval of established critics but few
writers have had to face such silly, waspish, and unfair
attacks as did the members of this gifted family. Sir Osbert
quotes a typical comment from a relation who wrote to a
friend, 'they are quite nice and amusing young people if

only they would not write '.[1] It was the implicit scorn of such comments (which were all carefully retailed to Sir George and Lady Ida by amiable mischief-makers) which was wounding.

The magnanimity and indeed the greatness of Sir Osbert are suggested by his refusal to be soured by these experiences. How many writers—Byron and even Pope suggest themselves—have corrupted some of their finest work by a natural longing to give blow for blow—to wipe out old wounds by giving a sudden and avenging stroke to an adversary, remembered but unworthy.

During the 1930's Sir Osbert published, in addition to *Miracle on Sinai*, three prose books which were not polemical or satirical. The first and most important was *Winters of Content*, 1932. This was a description of travel in Italy—a more mature development of his striking descriptive powers already shown in *Discursions*. The second was written with Miss Margaret Barton and was a history (with particular reference to architecture) of Brighton. This book illustrates the way in which Sir Osbert could forget old feuds and battles and concentrate on something—the appreciation of eighteenth and early nineteenth century architecture—which was at that time stirring the minds of enlightened men and women. At the end of the 1930's he published a delightful book of travel, based on a recent journey to China, called *Escape with Me!*

During the 1930's English writing was invaded (and well-nigh overwhelmed) by rude hordes of polemical authors : they had but a modicum of style, no imagination, and less wit, but they made up for these in vigour and confidence. They were perhaps to be compared with Carlyle without the genius. In novels, poems, and books of travel they called their fellow countrymen to battle on behalf of some ill-digested continental political dogma. Books about foreign lands were of course much favoured for this kind of writing and Sir Osbert neatly distinguished himself from

[1] *Laughter in the Next Room*, p. 62.

its exponents : 'Though I have long carried on a private, one-man campaign against stupidity, and the brutality and greed which are two of its symptoms, I am no soldier of a cause militant.'[1]

Those who seek a typical example of Sir Osbert's humour will find it in his account of the visit which he and some friends made, when they were staying in Peking, to the surviving eunuchs from the palace in the old imperial days. The Englishmen thought that they had reached the dwelling-place of these once influential neuters but, in-quiring in broken Chinese, they found that they were at a golf club whose members were not exactly flattered by the question. Subsequently they found the place they really wanted and it was characteristic of the malice of mankind (both caponized and natural) that the eunuchs' chief know-ledge of England (which they had acquired from a spiteful literary English traveller) lay in the fact that Bloomsbury was the great eunuch quarter of London.[2]

IV

The end of the 1930's saw the germ of the great auto-biography with which Sir Osbert has crowned his career. This is in five volumes. The first, *Left Hand! Right Hand!* was published in 1945 ; the second, *The Scarlet Tree*, in 1946 ; the third, *Great Morning*, in 1948 ; the fourth, *Laughter in the Next Room*, in 1949 ; and the fifth, *Noble Essences*, appeared in the autumn of 1950. In English litera-ture autobiography is perhaps a neglected form of art. There are of course plenty of autobiographies of a kind : these are for the most part written by public men, scribbled down, with little regard for grammar or what is likely to interest the reader, often merely a justification or explana-tion by people who think themselves ' misunderstood '. With such works Sir Osbert has nothing in common, though

[1] *Escape with Me!* p. vii.
[2] op. cit., p. 321.

in one respect these books of his are reminiscent of the great monumental biographies of eminent men which were greatly beloved by an earlier generation. These have of course been much ridiculed. Lytton Strachey, in the preface to *Eminent Victorians*, says ' they are as familiar as the cortège of the undertaker, and wear the same air of slow funereal barbarism '. Yet in their broad, leisurely canvas these old-fashioned biographies managed to show the temper and spirit of the age. That capacity for giving us the portrait of an epoch Sir Osbert shares with them, but his canvas gleams with the genius which illumines such immortal short autobiographies as Gibbon's *Autobiography*, Edmund Gosse's *Father and Son*, or W. H. Davies's *The Autobiography of a Super-Tramp*. Certain it is that future generations wishing to recapture the true spirit of English life in the great days before 1914 and in the tarnished, rather breathless years afterwards, will turn to Sir Osbert's graceful volumes.

More than 200 years ago Pope expressed a truth to whose force the great majority of successful writers would testify,

> True ease in writing comes from art not chance,
> As those move easiest who have learned to dance.[1]

These volumes of autobiography are particularly revealing of Sir Osbert's methods and show that he is a meticulously careful writer and a follower of Pope's precept. In *The Scarlet Tree* he makes the good point that an author, unlike the members of other professions, cannot leave his burdens behind in the way that other professional men can slam the office door, sign the last letter and fling it in the out-tray, or put off the spotless white equipment of the operating chamber. An author can take no holiday ; ' he must absorb and reflect the whole time '.[2] Confirmation of this will be found in an important and entertaining book called *Memoirs of an Aesthete*, by Mr. Harold Acton. At the end of the 1930's, when Sir Osbert was collecting

[1] *Essay on Criticism.*
[2] *The Scarlet Tree*, p. 33.

material for *Escape with Me!* he went out to China and he and Mr. Acton spent much time together ; the latter says, ' in the afternoons he pursued his leisurely promenades, laying in a store of images for that little masterpiece *Escape With Me!*'[1] Much of the preparatory work for his books was done at night or in the early morning when it was possible during the hours of wakefulness to think out a problem of composition which was proving obstinate. H. G. Wells once advised him, ' If you are in difficulties with a book, try the element of surprise. Attack it at an hour when it is not expecting it.'[2]

Readers of Anthony Trollope's *Autobiography* will remember how that greatly gifted and successful Victorian novelist confessed that much of his early writing was done in the railway train. He made for himself a special tablet and scribbled away his thoughts in pencil—not a contemptible physical performance when it is remembered that the trains of those days moved with the jolting clangour of a modern goods train. He provides the absolute contrast to Sir Osbert who could only write in solitude and goes so far as to hint that an author can only do himself full justice when he is writing for a spell not bounded by a fixed engagement at the end, and not liable to the invasions of even the best of friends. He wrote *Before the Bombardment* in a monastic cell in South Italy and *Escape with Me!* in a disused kitchen in Guatemala under the curious and rather hungry eye of a friendly vulture which hovered outside the window. But where Trollope and Sir Osbert are together is that both gave the public of their very best in spite of opposite methods. Trollope says that an author who writes his books badly because that way he can make his money faster is exactly the same as a fraudulent tradesman who sells shoddy for broadcloth.

The outstanding graces of Sir Osbert's writing are possibly more obvious in these volumes of autobiography

[1] *Memoirs of an Aesthete*, by Harold Acton. Methuen, 1948.
[2] *The Scarlet Tree*, p. 33.

than in some of his earlier books. His genial wit plays
through his mature writing with all its old quality and
originality as this one example shows. Being a delicate
baby he was twice baptized—once publicly and once
privately : this double sacrament he gives as the reason why
' the pomps and vanities of this wicked world ' have always
been especially dear to him.[1]

Nor will the reader fail to notice how the unrivalled
powers of description are maintained and even developed.
The short sentence which starts the first book is a masterpiece—bringing to life the surroundings of Renishaw. 'The
garden would be beautiful—and is beautiful—with no
flower blooming there.'[2] Again after reading all the
volumes the picture of the gamekeeper, Mark Kirkby,
stands out from Sir Osbert's description with the glowing
freshness of life.[3] Although, as Sir Osbert explains, he
himself was neither particularly proficient with the gun nor
enjoyed its use, he spent much of his time with the keeper
and delighted in his company. In his book he has caught
the interplay of this man's calling on his character with a skill
which is notable.

His more mannered and ceremonial descriptions are
equally good. For example, he was a spectator of the
astonishing scenes in London on Armistice Night in 1918.
Many observers—even trained newspaper men—were en-
grossed by the trivialities of the spectacle—the usually
demure ladies being warmly embraced by strangers, law-
abiding citizens flaunting the policeman's helmet, or clergy-
men in false noses. Not so Sir Osbert. He stood in
Trafalgar Square with Diaghilev and Massine, watching the
crowd which ' dashed like the waves of the sea against the
sides of the Square, against the railings of the National
Gallery, sweeping up so far even as beyond the shallow,

[1] *Left Hand! Right Hand!* p. 80.
[2] op. cit., p. 1.
[3] *Great Morning*, p. 99.

stone steps of St. Martin-in-the-Fields. The succeeding
waves flowed back, gathered impetus and broke again.
The northern character of the revellers—if they may be
described as that—was plain in the way they moved, in the
manner, for example, in which the knees were lifted, as in a
Kermesse painted by Breughel the Elder, as well as in the
flushed and intent faces. It was an honest, happy crowd,
good-natured, possessed of a kind of wisdom or philosophy,
as well as of a perseverance which few races knew : but it
had nothing of Latin grace. . . .'[1]

The close of the book is written in superbly measured
English. Looking towards the reader of future centuries,
Sir Osbert writes, ' I, a citizen of the Sunset Age, an Eng-
lishman who saw the world's great darkness gathering,
salute you, Stranger, across the Chasm. . . . What was the
world like before it fell . . . was there deep sorrow? No,
there was a peculiar sadness in the air, a feeling of hundreds
of days leading up to this particular day, and every now and
then the breath of a change to come as when the great airs
of summer move under August trees : only that and a surge
of vanity in man.'[2]

Some critics have found this ending to Sir Osbert's great
enterprise somewhat disappointing. It is suggested that he
should have ended on a top note of jubilation because so
much that he stood for both in literature and the arts has
now been approved by public opinion. Instead he prefers
to leave the reader with the possibility, with which he closes
the book, that ' there is little immediate future for mankind,
and that only many centuries hence the ruins will be un-
covered '. Yet this glimpse of prophetic sadness with which
the book ends is characteristic of one, who even as a young
man, was conscious that the selfishness and follies of mankind were destroying the world. When he was not

[1] *Laughter in the Next Room*, p. 4.
[2] op. cit., pp. 328–30.

twenty-five in the poem 'This Generation' he gave expression to this idea :

> Their youth was fevered—passionate, quick to drain
>   The last few pleasures from the cup of life
> Before they turn'd to suck the dregs of pain
>   And end their young-old lives in mortal strife.
> They paid the debts of many a hundred year
>   Of foolishness and riches in alloy.
> They went to death ; nor did they shed a tear
>   For all they sacrificed of love and joy.
> Their tears ran dry when they were in the womb,
> For, entering life—they found it was their tomb.

He might reasonably argue that he is only saying, as Matthew Arnold said before him :

> The bloom is gone, and with the bloom go I.

V

Whether the philosophy which lies behind this autobiography is needlessly melancholy or not, a further point about it ought to be made. Enshrined within it is one of the most sympathetic and most perfect biographies in the English language—the portrait of the writer's father, Sir George.

Sir George makes his first appearance on the second page of the first volume. He walks on to the stage with a characteristic lack of parade and ostentation. After describing Renishaw in the pompous month of August—and it is striking to notice in passing how Sir Osbert is fascinated by the potency of high summer for his book begins and ends with imagery from that season—he just slips in the sentence, 'And already, too, a tall man, fair and with a curious air of isolation, is out there upon the terraces '.[1]

Sir George was a fanatical admirer of everything medieval and the significance of the word ' already ' in the passage

[1] *Left Hand! Right Hand!* p. 2.

quoted lies in the fact that it was early morning : since medieval romances generally opened at dawn he was in the habit of being called at 5 a.m. in summer. Though he had been for many years a Conservative Member of Parliament and was clearly a shrewd man of business, his natural talents were vitiated by obstinate attachments to theories which were too often absurd. For example, he thought that backwardness in children was due to the fact that those coming from rich families had their food cut up for them long after they should have been cutting it up for themselves. Again he thought that his wife would have been well advised to let him choose her dresses ; he knew that they understood these things so much better in the middle ages and he considered that she would have looked charming in a delightful old leper's gown which he recalled having seen in Naples.[1]

He was preoccupied with himself. On one occasion he was elaborately preparing a practical joke for a luncheon guest who was to fall through a defective chair. Sir Osbert, as a child of four, put the chair in his father's place. His father sat down to luncheon eagerly watching his guest and fell through the chair. As he picked himself up he was heard to say, ' I might have most seriously injured my back '.[2] Later in life when he was staying in Italy he thought that he had forgotten the keys of his luggage. He broke open his own cases and his wife's : unluckily he included in the latter, two trunks of complete strangers who were just leaving the hotel. They were naturally indignant and made a great hubbub in which the hotel servants joined. Sir George locked himself in his bedroom and was heard saying, ' I am afraid that I really can't help other people's troubles '.[3] When he was a young man of twenty, somebody remembered him saying, ' I often suffer from nerve exhaustion myself but with me it takes the form of

[1] *The Scarlet Tree*, p. 55.
[2] *Left Hand ! Right Hand !* p. 161.
[3] *Laughter in the Next Room*, p. 273.

rheumatism in the deltoid muscle, and yields at once to Galvanism '.[1]

The reader will easily imagine that a man with these characteristics must, as a father, have proved remarkable. When Sir Osbert was eight his father sent him a letter from Nuremberg filled with abstruse details about the architecture, churches, and inhabitants of that city : the letter ended, ' I have bought an old picture in one of the curiosity shops for £40. It is dated 1480 and is painted by some painter of the Wohlgemuth school. W was Albert Dürer's master.'[2]

When he took his sons to stay in Venice he went to infinite pains to make certain that they were given rooms with diminutive Gothic windows from which in consequence most of the air and light were excluded. This was in illustration of his favourite theory that a view looked much more beautiful if it was seen from a window of unusual shape.[3]

In the portrait of his father Sir Osbert at once shows his humanity and sense of style. He had much justification for showing his father as an interesting survival of tyranny. A coarser-fibred writer like Sir Edmund Gosse did this successfully in *Father and Son*. Equally easy would it have been to depict Sir George as one more English eccentric. Sir Osbert, while showing all his father's almost limitless capacity for annoying his family, all his quirks and oddities, yet subtly discloses the pathos of the human being which they but thinly masked.

The following episodes are taken at random from the four books in illustration of this point. On Sir George's last visit to Renishaw he came into the house and his son asked him what he had been doing. ' Just been showing the gardener round the garden '[4] was the astonishing reply.

[1] *Great Morning*, p. 50.
[2] *The Scarlet Tree*. Appendix B.
[3] op. cit., p. 244.
[4] *Laughter in the Next Room*, p. 304.

And Sir Osbert gives it the necessary twist when he says that his father was in an obvious state of exhaustion. Sir George felt—and it is an extremely common failing—that he could always do things better than anybody else. ' Such a mistake not to ask me ' was his favourite catchword. Believing that he was infallible both in knowledge and experience he wore out his nervous energies in doing things which had best been left to others.

Even his more obviously funny remarks have their own decided pathos. They show what is perhaps the very core of tragedy—the clutching belief of a human being that its own natural importance and its own position in life entitle it to protection from indignities and discomforts. This was especially an attribute of the generation brought up amidst the security and assured comfort of English Victorian life. As an older man at Renishaw he would frequently be heard to say after dinner, ' I must ask anyone entering the house never to contradict me or differ from me in any way, as it interferes with the functioning of the gastric juices and prevents my sleeping at night '.[1]

His family, on occasions, could not prevent themselves from answering him back and when Sir Osbert did this when they were driving together his father said, ' I'm surprised. Rude to me in my own motor car.'[2]

Sir Osbert clearly shows his readers how his father's cleverness and kindliness—like shafts of sunlight—perpetually break through the mists of his oddity and selfishness. It was he who succeeded in dispelling his son's youthful terrors of hell by saying, ' My dear boy, if you go to hell you'll certainly find all the people you most admire there already—Wellington, Nelson, and the Black Prince—and they'll discover a way of getting you out of it soon enough '.[3] When his son was miserable at school he wrote to him to cheer him up. If the letter may not have had that

[1] *Laughter in the Next Room*, p. 252.
[2] *Great Morning*, p. 210.
[3] *The Scarlet Tree*, p. 86.

precise result the spirit behind it was good. ' The first
lesson of life is always to keep one's temper. In the seven
elections I have had at Scarborough, I learnt that a candidate
who loses his temper ever so little is throwing all his chances
away. If you study the husbands and wives you know, you
will find the one who keeps his or her temper settles everything.'[1]

Sir Osbert shows most clearly what was the tragedy of
his father's life. He was born to a great position, with great
possessions, in a prosperous civilization governed by certain
standards. During the span of years covered by his son's
autobiography he saw all these things eaten away and
undermined. Perhaps it would have been easier to bear if
it had been a great stroke of misfortune—a cataclysmic
disaster, swift and overwhelming, like the French Revolu-
tion : in fact it had more in common with the slow accumu-
lation of distress endured by the country in the Civil Wars,
which engendered something of the same intellectual
melancholy as was characteristic of Sir George. As Sir
Osbert builds up the story to its climax and pictures his
father old, alone in his Italian castle as the second world war
floods across the civilization of Europe, we recall the line
of G. K. Chesterton :

We only know the last sad squires ride slowly towards the sea.

That was in 1940 and in the profound picture of his
father which he has sought to draw—and has succeeded in
drawing—may lie the explanation of the disillusion and
sadness with which Sir Osbert closes the greatest of his
books.

VI

An editor of the Works of Dryden, who wrote in the
eighteenth century, observed in his introduction that he had
not exhausted his paper in tediously praising Dryden ; he
added that such a proceeding would be like the virtuoso who

[1] *The Scarlet Tree*, pp. 138-9.

insisted that nobody could see well except through his glass. His precept was wise. There is, however, one aspect of Sir Osbert's works which (if praise be deemed vulgar) certainly merits emphasis. That aspect is its almost astonishing variety. Poet, essayist, biographer, novelist—in all four capacities he achieves distinction. Of how many contemporary writers in any country could that be said ?

To these varied achievements he brings a mind of remarkable originality and versatility. He understands art ; he knows the tradition of Europe ; Italy is almost a second home to him, yet no one has their mind more firmly based on England and the English countryside. He has enjoyed the privacy of English social life no less than the festivities for, in spite of the hardships of the twentieth century, it could still be said, as King Leopold of the Belgians said over a century ago about England, ' there is hardly a country where such magnificence exists '. That magnificence Sir Osbert was peculiarly fitted to express. Nor is he without understanding of affairs. The unsuccessful Liberal candidate of 1918, the private citizen who played a not insignificant part in smoothing out the petty difficulties standing in the way of a solution of the General Strike, has plenty of shrewd observations—as well as severe criticism—on the subject of man's government of himself. He is above all a dissecter and critic of all those sloppy phrases by which men still try to comfort themselves, still seek to justify their particular brand of contemporary foolishness. He was quick to point out the peculiar grossness of the newspaper which cheered its readers after the end of the tortured years from 1939 to 1945 with the amazing news that the first fruits of victory were ' more sweets for the kiddies '. No man has done more to expose the rough brutality of English public school life, but when jokes about ' the old school tie ' were used as a sloppy witticism to cover countless things which never originated at school, Sir Osbert was quick to attack.[1]

[1] *Sing High ! Sing Low !* p. 26.

Although he is sometimes the critic of his age, and in his youth could be accused of a certain flippancy, he betrays on almost every page the diverse tastes and varied knowledge of a true man of letters. In the confused and panting decades of the mid-twentieth century he whispers to us the last enchantments of leisure ; he recalls to our often flustered minds the unruffled, spacious wisdom of an eighteenth-century gentleman discoursing on life : above all he can set on paper his opinions and experiences in a fashion which compel the attention and win the affection of those who read his books.

> Some chord in unison with what we hear,
> Is touch'd within us, and the heart replies.[1]

[1] Cowper : ' Winter Walk at Noon '.

OSBERT SITWELL

A

Select Bibliography

(Place of Publication London, unless otherwise stated.)

Bibliographies :

SITWELLIANA, 1915-1927 : Being a handlist of works of Edith, Osbert, and Sacheverell Sitwell. By Thomas Balston. Three portraits of the Authors by Albert Rutherston (1928).

Collected Editions :

THE COLLECTED SATIRES AND POEMS (1931).

SELECTED POEMS : OLD AND NEW (1943).

ALIVE—ALIVE OH ! and Other Stories (1947).
A collection of Stories from *Triple Fugue*, 1924, and *Dumb Animal*, 1930.

Separate Works :

TWENTIETH CENTURY HARLEQUINADE AND OTHER POEMS, by Edith and Osbert Sitwell. Oxford (1916). *Verse.*

ARGONAUT AND JUGGERNAUT (1919). *Verse.*

THE WINSTONBURG LINE. Three Satires (1920). *Verse.*
'A Certain Statesman'; 'More About Morale'; 'The Governess of Europe'.

AT THE HOUSE OF MRS. KINFOOT. Four Satires (1921).

WHO KILLED COCK ROBIN ? Reflections on Modern Poetry and its criticism (1921). *Criticism.*

OUT OF THE FLAME (1923). *Verse.*

TRIPLE FUGUE (1924). *Short Stories.*

WINTER THE HUNTSMAN (1924). *Poem.*

DISCURSIONS ON TRAVEL, ART AND LIFE. An Illustrated Book of Travel (1925). *Travel.*

C. R. W. NEVINSON (1925). *Criticism.*
In the Series Contemporary British Artists.

POOR YOUNG PEOPLE AND OTHER POEMS, by Edith, Osbert, and Sacheverell Sitwell (1925). *Verse.*

BEFORE THE BOMBARDMENT (1926). *Novel.*

ENGLAND RECLAIMED. A Book of Eclogues (1927). *Verse.*

ALL AT SEA. A Social Tragedy in Three Acts for First Class Passengers Only (1927). *Drama.*
In collaboration with Sacheverell Sitwell.

THE PEOPLE'S ALBUM OF LONDON STATUES. Described by Osbert Sitwell. Drawn by Nina Hamnett (1928).

THE MAN WHO LOST HIMSELF (1929). *Novel.*

MISS MEW. Stanford Dingley (1929). *Verse.*
Printed by Hon. Robert Gathorne-Hardy on his private press.

DUMB ANIMAL, AND OTHER STORIES (1930). *Short Stories.*

SOBER TRUTH. A collection of nineteenth-century episodes (strange occurrences) compiled and edited by Margaret Barton and Osbert Sitwell, with a Preface by Osbert Sitwell (1930).

THREE-QUARTER LENGTH PORTRAIT OF MICHAEL ARLEN. London and New York (1931). *Verse.*

VICTORIANA. A symposium of Victorian wisdom (strange sayings) compiled and edited by Margaret Barton and Osbert Sitwell (1931).

A THREE-QUARTER-LENGTH PORTRAIT OF VISCOUNTESS WIMBORNE (in verse). Cambridge (1931). *Verse.*

DICKENS (1932). *Criticism.*

WINTERS OF CONTENT. More Discursions on Travel, Art, and Life. An Illustrated Book of Travel (1932). *Essays.*
Reprinted with a new Preface, 1950.

MIRACLE ON SINAI. A Satirical Novel (1933). *Novel.*

BRIGHTON (1935). *Social history.*
In collaboration with Margaret Barton. On the social history of the town in the eighteenth and nineteenth centuries.

PENNY FOOLISH. A book of Tirades and Panegyrics (1935). *Essays.*

MRS. KIMBER (1937). *Verse.* With illustrations by Mary Kessell.

THOSE WERE THE DAYS. Panorama with Figures (1938). *Novel.*

DICKENS AND THE MODERN NOVEL—THE MODERN NOVEL : ITS CAUSE AND CURE.
In ' Trio. Dissertations on some Aspects of National Genius ', by Osbert, Edith, and Sacheverell Sitwell (1938). Delivered as the Northcliffe Lectures at the University of London in 1937. *Essays.*

ESCAPE WITH ME ! An Oriental Sketch-book (1939). *Travel.*

TWO GENERATIONS. A Double Biography. [Reminiscences of Georgiana Caroline Sitwell, afterwards Mrs. Campbell Swinton : Journal of Florence Alice Sitwell.] Edited, with a Preface, by Osbert Sitwell (1940). *Biography.*

OPEN THE DOOR ! (1941). *Short Stories.*

A PLACE OF ONE'S OWN. A Ghost Story (1941). *Short Novel.*

GENTLE CAESAR. A play in three acts (1942). *Drama.*
In collaboration with R. J. Minney.

A LETTTER TO MY SON (1944). *Essay.*

SING HIGH ! SING LOW ! (1944). *Essays.*

LEFT HAND ! RIGHT HAND ! Boston (1944). *Autobiography.*

THE SCARLET TREE. Being the second volume of 'LEFT HAND ! RIGHT HAND !' (1945). *Autobiography.*
First English edition, 1946.

THE TRUE STORY OF DICK WHITTINGTON. A Christmas Story for Cat Lovers (1945). *Short Story.*

THE NOVELS OF GEORGE MEREDITH, AND SOME NOTES ON THE ENGLISH NOVEL (1947). *Lecture.*
The English Association Presidential Address, 1947.

A FREE HOUSE ! OR, THE ARTIST AS CRAFTSMAN. Being the writings of Walter Richard Sickert. Edited by Osbert Sitwell (1947).

FOUR SONGS OF THE ITALIAN EARTH (1948). *Verse.*

GREAT MORNING. Being the third volume of 'LEFT HAND ! RIGHT HAND !' Boston (1947). *Autobiography.*
First English edition, 1948.

LAUGHTER IN THE NEXT ROOM. A continuation of 'LEFT HAND ! RIGHT HAND !' Boston (1948). *Autobiography.*
First English edition, 1949.

DEMOS THE EMPEROR. A secular oratorio (1949). *Poetry.*

DEATH OF A GOD (1949). *Stories.*

NOBLE ESSENCES. The final volume of 'LEFT HAND ! RIGHT HAND !' London (1950). *Autobiography.*

Critical and Biographical Studies :

THE THREE SITWELLS. A Biographical and Critical study, by R. L. Mégroz (1927).

FIVE NOVELISTS OF TODAY (No. 5 Osbert Sitwell), by R. L. Mégroz (1933).

Sir Osbert Sitwell's *Collected Poems and Satires* is published in a limited edition by Messrs. Duckworth at 63s. net, signed by the author. The same firm publish at 42s. net *The People's Album of London Statues* ; at 21s. net *Winters of Content and other Discursions on Mediterranean Art and Travel* ; at 8s. 6d. net *Before the Bombardment* and *Miracle on Sinai* ; at 7s. 6d. net *Selected Poems : Old and New* ; and at a florin *Who Killed Cock Robin ?*

Messrs. Macmillan publish Sir Osbert's Autobiography, *Left Hand! Right Hand!* in 5 vols. *Left Hand! Right Hand!* itself, *The Scarlet Tree* and *Great Morning* (the first three volumes) are published at 15s. net. *Laughter in the Next Room*, the fourth volume, is published at 18s. net, and the final volume, *Noble Essences*, at a guinea. The set of five volumes can also be obtained, specially boxed, at 84s. net. Messrs. Macmillan also publish the following: *A Free House!* at 25s. net ; *Escape with Me !* 16s. net. *Sing High ! Sing Low !* at half a guinea ; *Mrs. Kimber* and *Death of a God* at 8s. 6d. net, and *Demos the Emperor* at 2s. 6d. and 8s. 6d. net.

(All prices are subject to alteration without notice.)

INDEX TO ESSAYS AND SHORT STORIES

(The title in brackets indicates the volume title)

Adult Franchise for Domestic Animals (*Penny Foolish*)

Alive—Alive Oh ! (*Dumb-Animal*)

America Before the Fall (*Penny Foolish*)

Animals versus Children (*Penny Foolish*)

Arms and the Man (*Penny Foolish*)

Art of Pavel Tchelitchew, The (*Sing High ! Sing Low !*)

Arts of Reading and Writing : Their Future, The (*Penny Foolish*)

Ballet, The (*Penny Foolish*)

Banquets of Tantalus, The (*Sing High ! Sing Low !*)

Best Years of Life, The (*Penny Foolish*)

Champagne for the Old Lady (*Open the Door !*)

Charles and Charlemagne (*Dumb-Animal*)

Conspiracy of Dwarfs, The (*Sing High ! Sing Low !*)

Dead Heat (*Open the Door !*)

Death of a God (*Open the Door !*)

Defeat (*Open the Door !*)

Delights of Foreign Colonies, The (*Penny Foolish*)

Dogs (*Penny Foolish*)

Dumb-Animal (*Dumb-Animal*)

Echoes (*Dumb-Animal*)

Edwardians : The Rich Man's Feast, The (*Penny Foolish*)

Eighteenth Century Details (*Penny Foolish*)

Encounter with the Oxford Group Movement (*Penny Foolish*)

Eye within the Ear, The (*Sing High ! Sing Low !*)

Fortune Tellers (*Penny Foolish*)

Friends (*Penny Foolish*)

Friends and Enemies (*Penny Foolish*)

Friendship's Due (*Triple Fugue*)

Games (*Penny Foolish*)

Ghost in the Green Mask, The (*Penny Foolish*)

Glow-worm, The (*Open the Door !*)

Grain of Sand and a Grain of Salt, A (*Sing High ! Sing Low !*)

Greeting, The (*Triple Fugue*)

Happy Endings (*Dumb-Animal*)

Hints on Life (1) Manners (2) Success (*Penny Foolish*)

His Ship Comes Home (*Triple Fugue*)

Holiday Conversations (*Penny Foolish*)

Idyll Through the Looking-Glass (*Open the Door !*)

In Praise of Indolence (*Penny Foolish*)

Is Fascism British ? (*Penny Foolish*)

Let's Be All Alike ! (*Penny Foolish*)

Lewd Sing Cuckoo (*Penny Foolish*)

London (*Sing High ! Sing Low !*)

Long Journey (*Open the Door !*)

Love Bird, The (*Dumb-Animal*)

Lovers Meeting (*Open the Door !*)

Low Tide (*Triple Fugue*)

Machine Breaks Down, The (*Triple Fugue*)

Man who Drove Strindberg Mad, The (*Open the Door !*)

Messenger, The (*Open the Door !*)

More About Monkey Glands (*Penny Foolish*)

Municipal Rhapsody, An Idyll (*Sing High ! Sing Low !*)

Note on the Novel, A (*Penny Foolish*)

Old Worlds for New (*Sing High ! Sing Low !*)

On a Common Cold (*Penny Foolish*)

On Advice : It's giving and receiving (*Penny Foolish*)

On Anonymous Letters (*Penny Foolish*)

On Broadening the Mind (*Penny Foolish*)

On Centenaries (*Penny Foolish*)

On Cut Flowers (*Penny Foolish*)

On English Food (*Penny Foolish*)

One or Two Lives (*Penny Foolish*)

On Exhibitions (*Penny Foolish*)

On Fogs (*Penny Foolish*)

On Gardening (*Penny Foolish*)

On Health (*Penny Foolish*)

On Interior Decorators and Decoration (*Penny Foolish*)

On Prigs (*Penny Foolish*)

On Private Schools (*Penny Foolish*)

On Progress (*Penny Foolish*)

On Prophets and Prophecy (*Penny Foolish*)

On Public Schools (*Penny Foolish*)

On Sex (*Penny Foolish*)

On Snobs (*Penny Foolish*)

On Street Music (*Penny Foolish*)

On the Belittlement of the Great (*Penny Foolish*)

On the Burning of Books as Private Pastime and National Recreation (*Penny Foolish*)

On the Decay of Privacy (*Penny Foolish*)

On the Effect of Minding one's own Business (*Penny Foolish*)

On the Horror of Solitude (*Penny Foolish*)

On the Joys of a Telephone Exchange, and How to Depict Them (*Penny Foolish*)

On Words and Their Meaning (*Penny Foolish*)

Out of Season (*Penny Foolish*)

Picnics and Pavilions (*Sing High ! Sing Low !*)

Plague-Cart before Horse (*Open the Door !*)

Pompey and Some Peaches (*Open the Door !*)

Portrait of Lawrence (*Penny Foolish*)

Primavera (*Open the Door !*)

Red Folder, The (*Sing High ! Sing Low !*)

Roots of the Sole Arabian Tree (*Sing High ! Sing Low !*)

Rose by any other Name, A (*Sing High ! Sing Low !*)

Rules for Being Rude (*Penny Foolish*)

Save the Old School Tie ! (*Sing High ! Sing Low !*)

Shadow Play (*Open the Door !*)

Some Present Elements of Literary Corruption (*Penny Foolish*)

Still Life (1) Dining Room Piece (2) Box and Bottle (*Sing High !
   Sing Low !*)

Summer Palace, The (*Penny Foolish*)

Ta-ra-ra-boom-da-ay (*Penny Foolish*)

Thackeray and ' Vanity Fair ' (*Penny Foolish*)

That Flesh is Heir To (*Dumb-Animal*)

Thomas Rowlandson (*Sing High ! Sing Low !*)

Touching the Wood (*Open the Door !*)

Travellers' Tales (*Penny Foolish*)

Travelling Abroad (*Penny Foolish*)

Travelling by Boat (*Penny Foolish*)

Travelling by Train (*Penny Foolish*)

Triple Fugue (*Triple Fugue*)

True Lovers' Knot (*Open the Door !*)

Victorianism, An English Disease (*Penny Foolish*)

What it Feels Like to be an Author (*Sing High ! Sing Low !*)

White Man's Burden, The (*Penny Foolish*)

Woman Who Hated Flowers, The (*Open the Door !*)